A Young Slugger's Guide to HITTING

Building a Solid Foundation for Baseball and Softball Players

CHRISTOPHER ALLEN

© 2018 WHEELHOUSE BASEBALL CLINIC, INC.

ISBN-13: 978-0692103296 (Christopher Allen)

ISBN-10: 0692103295

All rights reserved. No part of this book may be reproduced or transmitted in any form or by any means without written permission from the author.

Always consult your physician before beginning any exercise program. This general information is not intended to diagnose any medical condition or to replace your healthcare professional. Consult with your healthcare professional to design a customized exercise program. If you experience any pain with these exercises, stop and seek medical attention immediately.

DEDICATION

This book is dedicated to everyone who has had a hand in shaping my career. I am thankful for everyone who served as a teammate of mine. I am especially grateful for the players and parents that train with me today.

Specifically, I want to thank my parents, Mitchell and Linda Allen. Their dedicated efforts went from coaching to running the leagues to managing the concession stands. They built our baseball community from the ground up. I did not appreciate my parent's efforts at the time, but now as I am making a career in baseball, I have extreme gratitude for the life lessons their efforts have taught me.

To my sons, Mason, Jackson, and Harrison, who have taught me the importance of being a good coach and a good dad. Being the coach's kid is the hardest job on the field. I am so proud of my boys for their hard work and dedication to each of their own talents, both on and off the field.

To Mary and Zoey, thank you for helping me down the final stretch of this project. The clarity of life that you have provided has paved the way for all of my projects to come to life, thank you.

To Dain Wilson, thank you for all the time we spent together. Thank you for trusting me with your game and allowing me to develop my coaching style through years of hard work.

To my current athletes, thank you for putting your trust in me. I am honored to be the tour guide on your baseball journey. I cannot wait to see what you will achieve in life.

TABLE OF CONTENTS

Preface.. vii

Introduction 1

Chapter 1: Bat Selection 5

Chapter 2: Bat Regulations 9

Chapter 3: Grip.. 15

Chapter 4: Alignment................................ 17

Chapter 5: Stance 21

Chapter 6: Load And Explode 25

Chapter 7: Swing Sequence 27

Chapter 8: Common Flaw Series................. 43

Chapter 9: Mental Preparation 53

Chapter 10: Practice Habits....................... 57

Chapter 11: Training Aids.......................... 59

Conclusion 61

Preface

Building better baseball players has been my passion for many years. I want to help the game that has shaped my life into what it is today.

The Young Slugger's Hitting System is a simple and deliberate system to address the many flaws seen by the dozens of young sluggers who pass through my building week after week. The techniques in this book will minimize the unnecessary movements pertaining to many sluggers. This system is about reducing the number of variables that cause poor swing mechanics. My goal is for children to experience the game in a simple way, and develop their own love for the game. My hope is to help hitters find success earlier than most, and therefore, have a greater likelihood of playing baseball throughout life.

Every swing is a journey that must be developed over time, and will vary slightly based on individual strength, athleticism, work ethic and commitment to excellence. The beauty of baseball is that every lesson we learn on the field will transfer to any life experience you will encounter off the field.

As you work through the Young Slugger's Hitting System, please practice patience as it will take time to build up to be the hitter you want to be. Do not let your struggles stifle you, let them fuel you.

> *"It takes a lot of work to become an overnight success."*

PREFACE

Age 5 **Age 8** **Age 10** **Age 11**

I started training Dain Wilson when he was eleven years old. Dain was on the verge of quitting baseball due to his lack of success at the plate. He loved the game, but could not handle the constant failures game after game. We developed a plan and went to work. We spent many hours working, learning, experimenting and found success. Then we built on that time and time again. It was not an upward road to success but a winding, bumpy journey to excellence. The system I developed through working with Dain has gone on to build swings for hundreds of successful hitters. The only hitters who do not succeed with this process are those who do not have the work ethic to succeed.

PREFACE

Age 12

Age 13

Age 14

Age 15

Dain is now sixteen years old, and is an absolute beast at the plate. I expect him to be one of the highest rated catchers in the country by the end of his senior season. Our motto was, "Hard work works."

The best time to plant a tree is 20 years ago.
The second best time is now.
—Chinese proverb

Introduction

The purpose of this book is to give coaches and parents a head start on building a fundamental swing for their young slugger. I want children to enjoy the game and find their own love for the game. My hope is that this book will allow them to find success much earlier than learning things the hard way. I hope together, we can simplify the movements and manage our expectations. As a result, we are all successful, regardless of our definition of success.

For the parents that read this book and apply these principles, I urge you to practice patience. Remember that your young slugger will grow and develop over time. Do not rush this process. It is simply that, a process. If you commit to the process, the results will take care of themselves. Allow them time to grow, allow them to fail, allow them to seek and find their own way. It is their failures and ability to learn from them that will shape them for life.

On the next page is a short story that was shared with me that will put the pressure, we as parents, put on our kids and the impact it has on them.

Allow them time to grow, allow them to fail, allow them to seek and find their own way.

INTRODUCTION

A mother was making breakfast for her teenage ball player. Suddenly, the boy runs into the kitchen screaming. "Careful, Careful!" Put in butter! Oh my goodness! Put in more butter! You are cooking too many eggs at once. Too Many! Turn them! Turn them now! We need more butter! What are you doing? Where are we going to get more butter? They are going to stick!

Careful!...Careful! I said be careful! You NEVER listen to me when you are cooking! Never! Turn Them! Hurry Up! Are you crazy? Have you lost your mind? Do not forget the salt. You always forget the salt. Use the salt. USE THE SALT! The Salt. S.A.L.T.

The mother after trying to keep up with his demands finally had enough and snapped back. "What is wrong with you son? Do you not think I know how to make eggs?"

The son calmly replied, "Yes mother, I know you can make eggs. I wanted to show you what it feels like when you yell at me during my baseball games..."

INTRODUCTION

To my fellow coaches, please do not over-coach. Allow your players to work and feel their way through this game. Guide them, motivate them, inspire them and watch them grow. The principle concept I teach my players is "If you can feel it, we can fix it."

I teach my players to find their own feel and make their own adjustments. The more control they have of the process, the more enjoyment they will find.

The most impact I have with my players is not telling them what to do, but by asking them why they made a movement or decision. Then we work backwards to understand why we are making each action, or why we do each little aspect of the game. When they understand why, they are much more likely to commit to the task I am trying to teach. When they are more committed, we both win!

I want to stress that there is no "perfect way" to become a great hitter. All hitters go about it in their own way. This book will help you build a productive swing. It will get a young slugger started off with minimal movement, consistent bat plane and consistent contact.

I will walk you through the entire process I use when I start my young sluggers off from bat selection to a complete swing. As I stress with all of my players, each of these steps are equally important. You must treat each step as a brick in your foundation, and lay each one as perfectly as a brick can be laid. If you do that with each brick, at the end of the bricks will be a beautiful wall.

The principles taught here are based on years of research, trial and error, and on the field results. I have taken young sluggers of all ages, sizes and ability levels and guided them toward success. Each player or coach who has implemented this system has found their teams winning at a much more consistent level. When I first used this system on my son's 8U team, they were ranked second in the nation in the USSSA Power Rankings. While that is not a ranking to brag about, it will put things in perspective at how dominate your team can be when your entire roster can rake.

INTRODUCTION

Trust the process!
The results take care of themselves.

Regardless of your slugger's age or ability level, these core principles are designed to get new hitters started in the game of baseball. As they get more strength, coordination and understanding of the game, they should seek more advanced principles. They are posted on my website www.wheelhousebaseballclinic.com under Training Drills.

It's not about being right.
It's about getting it right.

Chapter 1

Bat Selection: Your First Real Investment in Their Game

The first step in the Young Slugger's Guide to Hitting is choosing the right bat. I will spend a lot of time on this section, as this is the number one question I see from parents. The most common complaint I hear from parents is difficulty in buying the right bat. They admit to having limited knowledge or understanding of the rules and regulations. They often end up buying a bat, and trying it before they realize it is too long or too heavy. This leads into purchasing multiple cheap bats in an attempt to save money. Let's work on getting this part right to get the best bat for your budget.

Many bats are sold under the "advice" of the kid working in the sporting goods section of your local store. They may not even be a baseball player, or have any knowledge of the game. I get parents on a weekly basis who were guided toward a bat purchase, only to find out that it is not legal for their kids' level of play. This frustration in parents pushed them away from the game for financial reasons, simply because they were not prepared to make an educated decision.

Improper bat selection will lead to poor movement patterns, poor practice habits and poor results. This step, if not taken carefully, could ruin your young slugger's confidence and possibly drive them away from the game. I will offer some simple solutions to help guide you down the road to make the right bat selection for your young slugger.

CHAPTER 1: BAT SELECTION: YOUR FIRST REAL INVESTMENT IN THEIR GAME

Q If my son is on the fence between a 28 inch or 29 inch bat, should I buy the bigger bat so he can grow into it?

A A heavier bat will not increase their success. It will only impede their growth.

The first step to parents overwhelmed with bat selection is to understand the primary goal of your young slugger's bat. Your child needs a bat that they can swing hard, while maintaining balance and acceleration through impact with the ball. For kids under the age of nine I recommend a bat weighing twelve to sixteen ounces. A heavier bat will not increase their success. It will only impeed their growth.

My universal answer for young slugger's is to get a bat they can swing hard. A lighter bat is easier to control and keep on plane. I encourage you to start as light as you can and only go heavier when the rules require you to do so.

Personally, I used a 32 inch bat through my entire high school and college career. Even today, as I hit with my teams or do live demonstrations, you will see me swinging a 32 inch 29 ounce bat, simply because it feels good.

Many Major Leaguers use bats from 32 inches to 35 inches. The legendary Tony Gwynn used a 32 inch bat for the bulk of his Hall of Fame career.

Below is a chart of the most common bat lengths that I am seeing in my facility with those young sluggers who are finding constant success. This is by no means the rule, but merely a guide to point you in the right direction. If you are unsure, please seek advice from a qualified source or ask Coach Chris for a personal recommendation though Twitter #askcoachchris.

Most popular bat lengths by age							
Age	5 to 7	8 to 9	10	11 to 12	13 to 14	15 to 16	17 & up
Length	24-26"	26-29"	28-31"	30-31"	31-32"	32-33"	32-34"

CHAPTER 1: BAT SELECTION: YOUR FIRST REAL INVESTMENT IN THEIR GAME

Now that you have the right size window to select from, let us explore the various materials that you will discover in your search for the right bat. I will explain each one so that you can have an understanding of their properties.

Aluminum

- Have a distinct "ping" sound on contact
- Do not require a break-in period to obtain peak performance
- At peak performance right out of the wrapper
- Usually come with a one-year manufacturer warranty
- Susceptible to denting toward the end of their lifespan

Composite

- Have a "thud" sound on contact
- May require a break-in period of about 50-500 swings from a tee or soft-toss
- Susceptible to cracking toward the end of their life spans
- Composed of carbon, glasses, and Kevlar fibers that are embedded in a plastic resin

Hybrid

- Offer a lightweight composite handle with an alloy barrel, which is designed to reduce handle vibration

Wood

- Produced from a variety of trees: Maple, birch, and ash are the most popular
- Offer that classic and authentic feel but are more susceptible to cracking and breaking in comparison to aluminum and composite
- Seldom used by youth due to the expense and frequency of breaking

Wood Composites

- Comprised of multiple types of wood or different wood blends, and are not a natural piece of wood as a typical wood bat is
- Because these are not natural cuts of wood, leagues do require these to show certifications to be legal for play
- Typically more durable than a natural cut wood bat

Bamboo

- Look and perform like a wood bat, but bamboo is technically a grass
- Bamboo billets are pressed together to make a single bat and are often more durable than a natural cut wood bat

CHAPTER 1: BAT SELECTION: YOUR FIRST REAL INVESTMENT IN THEIR GAME

A few other variations that you will encounter

One-piece Bats

- Stiffer in comparison to a two-piece bat and will offer less flex during a player's swing
- Designed for more advanced hitters with above average swing speeds

Two-piece Bats

- Offers more flex during a player's swing: This causes a whip-like action through the swing zone and results in more inertia and power.
- Designed for smaller hitters who need the added pop of the improved bat speed, because the handle is separate from the barrel
- Tend to help mitigate felt vibration on mishit balls

Balanced Bats

- Will have their weight distributed evenly throughout the entire length of the bat
- Geared more towards average players with average or slower bat speeds

End-loaded Bats

- Have a portion of their weight focused towards the end of the barrel
- Designed for power hitters or those with above average swing speeds

#askcoachchris

Q What is the hottest bat?

A Please use this as a general guideline to get you started. Find a bat they feel comfortable with and go. As your child progresses, your coach or hitting instructor should be able to guide you down a more customized bat selection.

Chapter 2
Bat Regulations

Each league will have rules that change city-to-city and state-to-state. I would recommend that you call your league director to determine the official governing body before starting any search for an expensive bat.

Each bat will have required markings that must be met showing they have been tested and approved by the governing bodies of the leagues. These markings are permanently stamped on every bat. As you enter the higher levels of competition, these bats will be inspected before every game. I will provide a short summary and sample of the most common stamps we see here in the United States.

#askcoachchris

Q How do I know what regulations apply to me?

A I recommend that you call your league director or coach to determine the official governing body before purchasing an expensive bat.

CHAPTER 2: BAT REGULATIONS

BBCOR: Bat-Ball Coefficient of Restitution

This certification is the standard that regulates the overall performance of *adult bats used by high school and collegiate players*. BBCOR measures the trampoline effect of the bat.

USSSA BPF 1.15

BPF means "Bat Performance Factor," which measures how fast the ball comes off the bat.

1.15 is the standard for youth baseball bats.

USSSA BPF 1.20

Bat Performance Factor for Slow Pitch and Fast Pitch softball governed leagues.

SSUSA BPF 1.21

Bat Performance Factor for Slow Pitch senior softball leagues such as SSUSA.

CHAPTER 2: BAT REGULATIONS

NEW NATIONAL BAT STANDARD
STARTING JANUARY 1, 2018

Starting in 2018, USA Baseball, the national governing body for the sport of baseball in the U.S., in conjunction with participating national member organizations will adopt a new method for measuring bat performance in the testing of youth bats. The new USA Baseball bat standard (USABat), which will apply to bats that are classified below the National Collegiate Athletic Association (NCAA) and National Federation of State High School Associations (NFHS) level of play, will be implemented on January 1, 2018, allowing the bat manufacturers sufficient time to bring these bats to the marketplace.

There will be no immediate change to youth baseball organizations' bat rules. All bats, currently accepted for the respective leagues, remain permissible through December 31, 2017. Each participating national member organization will incorporate the new standard into their rules for the 2018 season and will begin, with this announcement, to inform their membership of the USABat standard.

As of May 2017, the following organizations are participating (in alphabetical order):

- American Amateur Baseball Congress (AABC)
- Amateur Athletic Union (AAU)
- Babe Ruth Baseball/Cal Ripken Baseball
- Dixie Youth Baseball
- Little League Baseball
- PONY Baseball

Their reasoning behind the new standard is that USA Baseball believes that a wood-like performance standard will best provide for the long-term integrity of the game. The new standard will not have a drop-weight limit, so young players can use bats made with lightweight materials.

CHAPTER 2: BAT REGULATIONS

Softball Bats

In the softball arena, there are many governing bodies and numerous variations. Here is the listing for each class as well as sample images of each.

USSSA:
United States Specialty Sports Association

ASA:
Amateur Softball Association

ISF:
International Softball Federation

NSA:
National Softball Association

The drop

Along with the official approval stamp, there will also be length, weight and barrel diameter listed on each barrel.

Length-to-Weight ratio is also known as "drop." The "drop" is the weight of the bat (in ounces) subtracted from the length (in inches). This is the same as the length-to-weight ratio. What this term defines is the difference between the length of the bat (in inches) and the weight of the bat (in ounces). The larger the "drop", the lighter the bat. Most bats come in a variety of length-to-weight ratios varying anywhere between a -3 to a -14. I recommend using the shortest bat for their height with the largest possible length-to-weight ratio.

#askcoachchris

Q What is drop?

A If you have a -10 length-to-weight ratio and a 26 inch bat, you will subtract ten from the inches and get the weight of 16 ounces.

26 (bat length) **- 10** (the drop) **= 16** (bat weight)

CHAPTER 2: BAT REGULATIONS

Diameter

Youth bats will come in multiple diameters. Various governing bodies often regulate these diameters as well. I recommended that you consult your local league officials to determine your governing body.

TEE BALL

- -10.5 to -14 length-to-weight ratio with a 2 ¼" barrel diameter
- Designed for youth players who are hitting baseballs or softballs placed on a tee

YOUTH

- -9 to -13 length-to-weight ratio with a 2 ¼" barrel diameter
- Designed for youth players required to use a 2 ¼" barrel diameter

JUNIOR BIG BARREL

- -9 to -12 length-to-weight ratio with a 2 ¾" barrel diameter
- Designed for players who are in machine pitch or coach pitch leagues with pitch velocities less than 40 mph

BBCOR

- -3 length-to-weight ratio with a 2 ⅝" barrel diameter
- Traditionally, required for high school/college level

FASTPITCH SOFTBALL

- -8 to -13 length-to-weight ratio with a 2 ¼" barrel diameter
- Designed for fastpitch softball players of all ages

SLOW PITCH SOFTBALL

- -3 to -8 length-to-weight ratio with a 2 ¼" barrel diameter
- Most common weights are 26, 27, 28, and 30 ounces

Chapter 3
Grip: Let Nature Lead the Way

The next step to the Young Slugger's Hitting System is grip. For younger players, I prefer to teach a natural grip, also known as a 10-finger grip. I want the grip to be comfortable and relaxed.

There are other options out there, but I stress the 10-finger grip for my younger hitters due to its simplicity. A standard 10-finger grip will have the hands double stacked. Right-handed hitters will start with their left hand on the bottom and the right hand on top. They should have their "big knuckles" on their right hand and their "door knockers" on their left hand lined up with each other. This process will be reversed for left handed hitters.

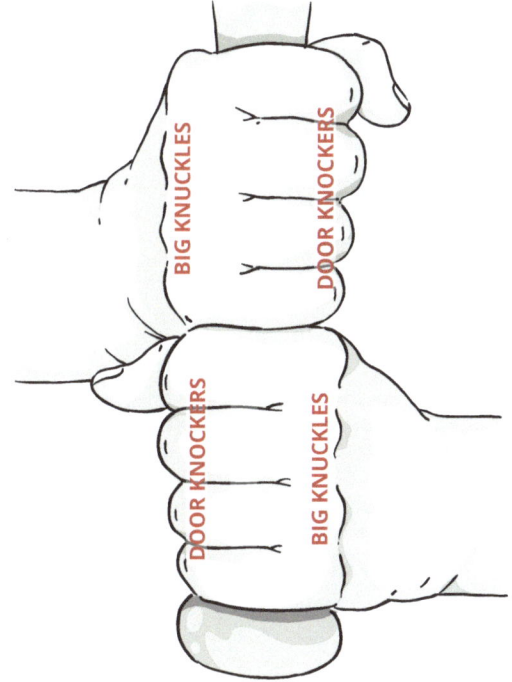

There are other grip options used by elite hitters, but I will not include those here as not to confuse the young sluggers. As your slugger matures, they will learn to experiment and will try different grips that are more comfortable or offer variable levels of performance. This chapter is short for a reason.

Please do not over complicate this step.

Chapter 4
Alignment: Foundation for Success

The next step in the journey of the Young Slugger's Guide to Hitting is the alignment process. As with building any strong structure, it must start with a strong foundation. I teach my young sluggers from the bottom up, because most swing flaws are caused by poor lower half movement patterns.

Tee placement

One of my biggest complaints about tee ball programs is the uninformed use of the tee. Every tee ball program, I have ever seen, are using the traditional hitting tee with the ball centered over home plate.

You will notice in the image that the ball is centered over home plate.

My issue with this style of tee is that kids are taught to take their stance directly even with the plate, therefore causing their targeted impact directly across from their midline. This will create a jamming effect, and will teach improper impact positions. This means the hitters are making impact at a less efficient position, which creates soft ground balls, groundouts and a lack of enjoyment for parents and children. If you stumble across a tee ball game, make note of the hitters' position in relation to the tee and the direction of their ground balls.

CHAPTER 4: ALIGNMENT: FOUNDATION FOR SUCCESS

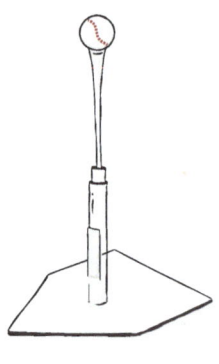 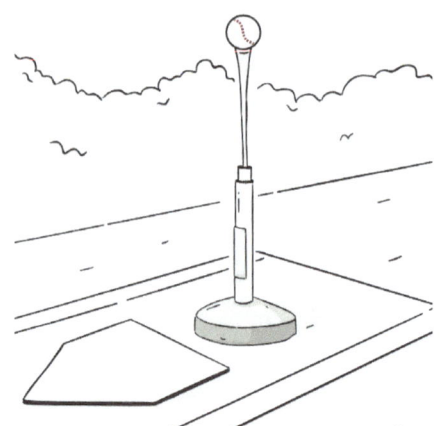

INCORRECT: Tee centered on home plate

CORRECT: Tee in front of home plate

The ideal impact points are referenced in the figure below. The white baseballs are the ideal impact points for right-handed hitters. You will notice how far in front of home plate an inside pitch is actually struck. I use these five positions while teaching my hitters. I place the tee in each location, so they can get the feel for creating the right swing for each pitch. These images are based on the Young Slugger's Hitting System alignment process. The ideal impact position for hitters off of live pitching will be anywhere from 6-18 inches in front of home plate.

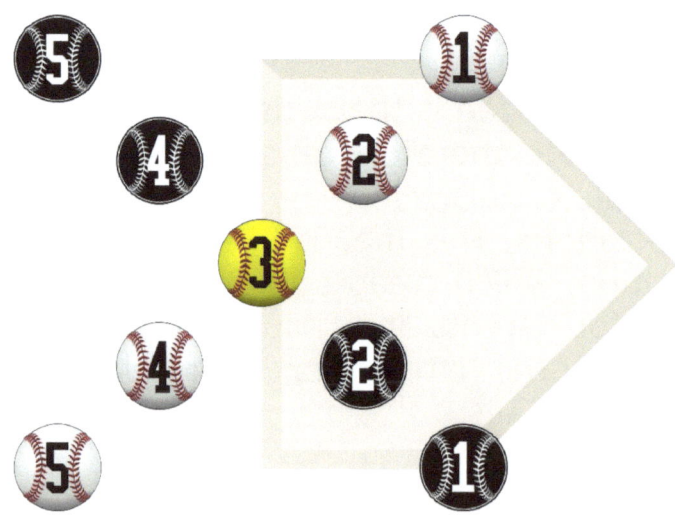

CHAPTER 4: ALIGNMENT: FOUNDATION FOR SUCCESS

The black baseballs are the ideal impact points for left-handed hitters. The yellow ball is position three, which is the ideal position for both right and left-handed hitters to hit a pitch right down the middle.

Foot placement

In order to overcome a young sluggers natural tendency I want to share my alignment process and why I use this method.

1. I ask my hitters to grab a bat, step up and prepare to hit. I make a mental note of their foot placement.
2. I ask them to step back 4-5 steps and repeat step one. If they can replicate their placement, I ask them why they like that location.

Most sluggers step with no regard for the depth in the box, distance from the plate or the dozens of other factors in play.

I have my players use the back corner of home plate as their reference point. This is where we start our alignment process, by placing our lead foot (front foot or foot closer to the pitcher) at the back corner of home plate.

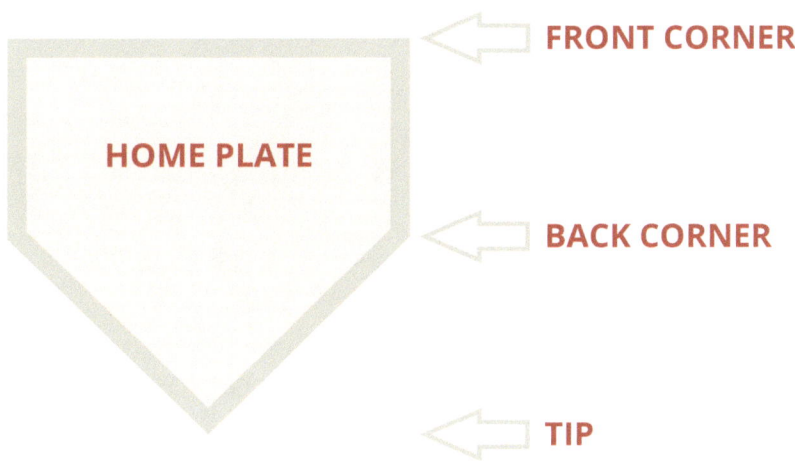

Chapter 5
Stance

I teach my hitters to stand with their feet just outside shoulder width apart, where they can transfer their weight forward and backward without losing balance. We will often get a little wider, if needed, to create a solid foundation. The stance is the element of the swing where I like to allow my hitters to find what is comfortable.

If the sluggers have trouble with the alignment process I have them place their feet together. I place a ball on the outside of each foot. I then have them step up and over each ball by saying step-step. This often gives them the visual and physical feedback to get their feet outside their shoulders, which feels balanced and comfortable.

CHAPTER 5: STANCE

Building your stance

For my young sluggers we start with this process.

Left-handed hitter:

Step 1. We place our left foot even with home plate, even with the back corner of the plate.

Step 2. Place your right foot directly behind your left foot, standing heel to toe.

Step 3. Leave your right foot planted, and take your left foot and step backwards towards the catcher.

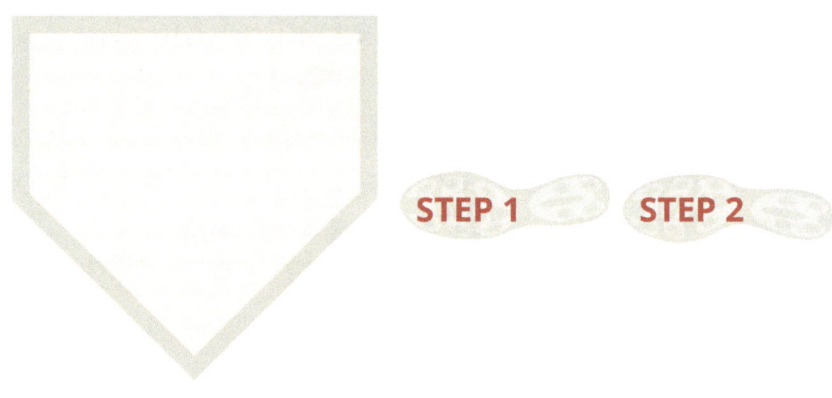

LEFT-HANDED HITTER

CHAPTER 5: STANCE

Right-handed hitter:

Step 1. Place our right foot even with home plate, even with the back corner of the plate.

Step 2. Place your left foot directly behind your right foot, standing heel to toe.

Step 3. Leave your left foot planted, and take your right foot and step backwards towards the catcher.

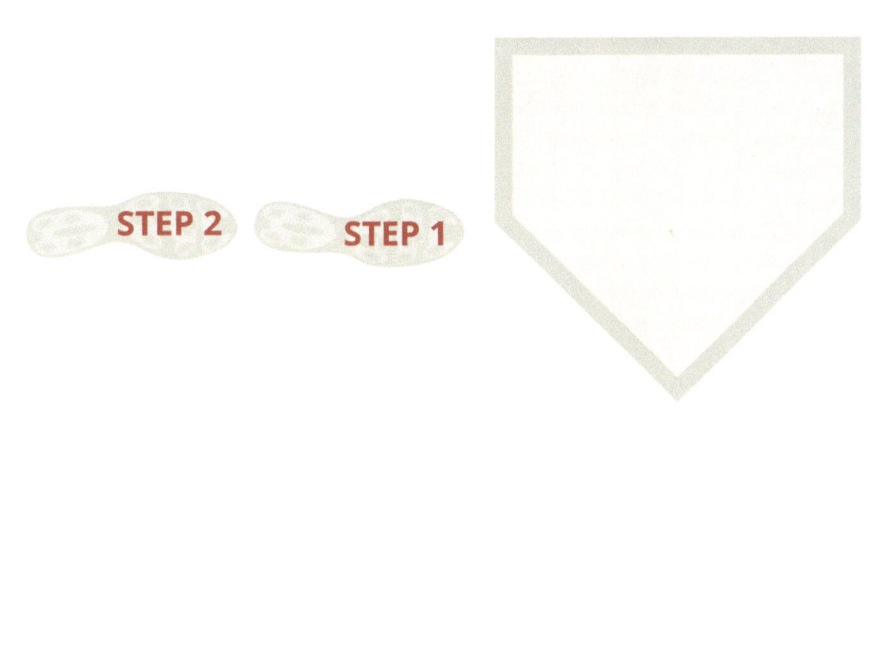

RIGHT-HANDED HITTER

CHAPTER 5: STANCE

Once you have the alignment process established for your young slugger, it must be repeated time and time again. If you ensure they have proper alignment every single time, then the remainder of our building blocks will fall into place.

I have my sluggers repeat this process after every 2-3 swings to ensure they understand the importance of it. Once a young slugger steps to the plate, this is where the real keys to my coaching cues come in handy. This lesson often goes untaught, and really eliminates many issues down the road. When a slugger gets frustrated or overwhelmed, a simple coaching cue of "RESET" will help them clear their head and get their mind focused on the fundamentals.

#askcoachchris

Q What is the cue to help them with this process?

A I use the cue "RESET" to have my players step out and repeat the steps every five swings until it becomes a habit.

Chapter 6
Load And Explode

Nearly every young hitter that comes to me for lessons is an arm swinger. They have not learned how to utilize their lower half to create rotational power for their swing.

I ask players to "press down" on their back leg, and show them how to push on the instep rather than the outside of the foot. This creates ground force that adds some pop to their swing as they rotate out of that stance into the swing. I tell them to push into the ground and use that leg to launch them forward, as they rotate to contact.

I ask the kids to "load," and I check them for balance by giving them a gentle nudge. If they lose their balance, we widen their stance to get a larger base. I tell the kids to think like a tree. A big strong tree has a large base and a small tree has a narrow base. If the wind is blowing hard, which one is the most stable?

I teach the kids to keep their weight on the inside of their back leg, pressing down into their instep rather than shifting their weight all the way back. I teach them to load into their instep and explode out of that with the back leg, as they rotate their hips to contact.

The last thought I want my hitters to have is to rotate through contact. I ask them to turn their back hip pocket towards the pitcher during their swing. This cue helps them rotate their hips through the hitting zone. I use

CHAPTER 6: LOAD AND EXPLODE

common terms to create different cues for each player. Some of the kids' favorites are "turn like a tornado" or "turn your booty". Whatever it takes to make them smile and understand the movement.

This is often the most difficult step for training. I will share several of my analogies for parents to use.

One of my favorites is to ask the slugger if they have ever punched their brother or sister. I then ask them to get in their hitting stance (with no bat), have them take their top hand, and punch my hand in front of the plate. I ask them to punch hard, and hold their fist in my hand and press. They will use their legs to generate power, and you can show them the connection to their back leg and the leverage they create with it.

#askcoachchris

Q How do you teach power?

A I teach efficiency. Power is the result of an efficient swing.

Chapter 7
Swing Sequence

As a coach, I have used video for analyzing all aspects of the game. I found it useful in helping my players understand their flaws. I have found that it helps hitters make improvements when they can see it and feel it. I use video to assess pitchers, hitters and even position players.

When the players see their actions, they are often enlightened as to the flaws in their movements and much more adaptive to change. The growing nature of technology in our game and the fact that nearly every player over the age of ten has their own phone, technology is the future. I am going to talk about the importance of video, and how simple the video analysis process can be when using the Young Slugger's Hitting System.

During the development of this Young Slugger's Hitting System, I have identified a series of checkpoints in the swing. Through years of research, I have identified these checkpoints in all of the games' top hitters. The most fastinating feature of these checkpoints is that they are common among the games' greats over many decades. I found that elite hitters, regardless of the generation, would hit these checkpoints on nearly every successful swing. After digging deep in the video archives, I could not find a successful hitter who operated significantly outside of these checkpoints. I also found many commonalities in the swing of these elite level hitters, and the swings of my successful youth hitters. It seems that when hitters hit these checkpoints on a consistent basis, they are more successful.

CHAPTER 7: SWING SEQUENCE

While developing this list of checkpoints, I have identified a series of flaws or tendencies of those hitters who struggle. I have identified over a dozen flaws that I repeatedly see in my young or unsuccessful hitters. These flaws will be discussed in detail in Chapter 8.

Below, I will explain the virtual checkpoints I have identified, and I will list them in sequence as they appear. I will explain the sequencing of the swing, and why each of these checkpoints is significant. I will walk you through each step of my evaluation process, and explain why I find value in evaluating each step of the swing sequence.

The checklist I use during my live lessons, or video analysis work, is a process. I have developed this process through years of evaluating swings, and helping players take their game to the next level. My process is very deliberate. I take great pride in my attention to detail which served me well as a former law enforcement officer. It is no surprise that my philosophy of "everything matters" is used during this process. The foundation of this philosophy is simple. If something is worth doing, it is worth doing to perfection. The swing is no different. I scrutinize each step in the swing that I have identified during slow motion video analysis.

The road to success and the road to failure are almost the exact same.

Do not expect this process to be quick and easy. It is a process, love the process and the results will take care of themselves.

CHAPTER 7: SWING SEQUENCE

Q: What kind of camera do you use to record swings?

A: I use a series of cameras for my evaluations such as HitTrax VCAM feature, Go Pro Cameras synced with the Coaches Eye application and my iPad Pro. The iPad Pro is my most portable and it has 240 frames per second. It or any smartphone with 30-60 frames per second will give you what you need to successfully evaluate your swing.

#askcoachchris

Over the last three years, I have been studying swings of hitters from multiple generations. Regardless of the generation, I have found many commonalities in the swings of great hitters. While they each have their own unique features, the swing sequence of any successful hitter follows these checkpoints consistently.

CHAPTER 7: SWING SEQUENCE

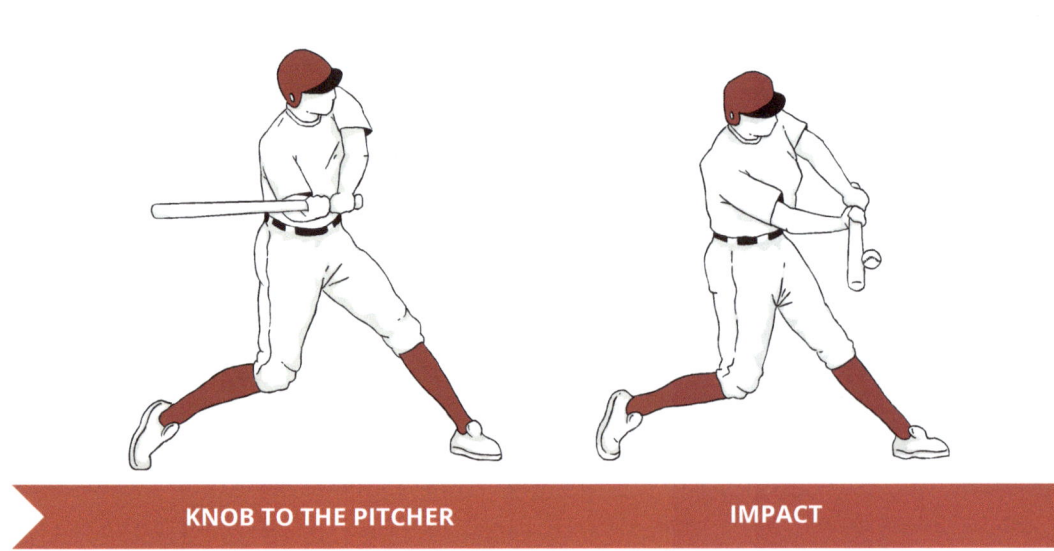

CHAPTER 7: SWING SEQUENCE

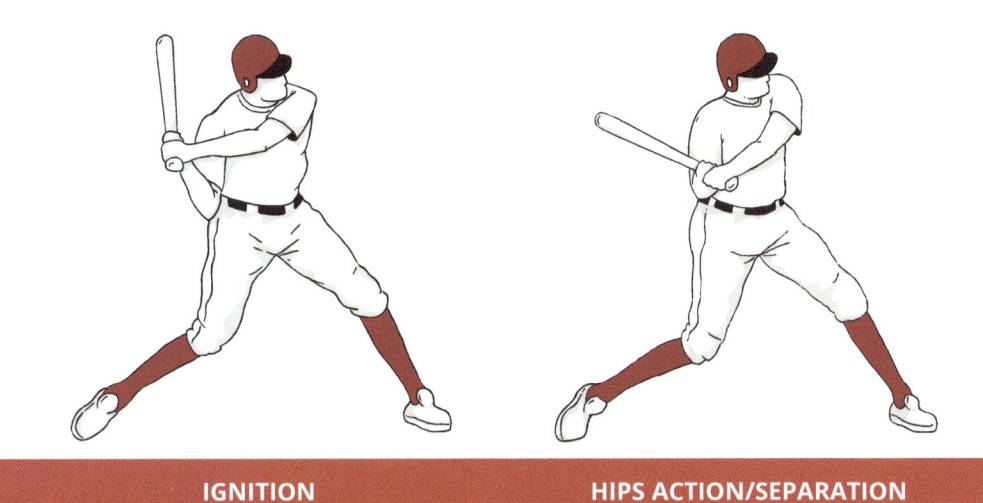

IGNITION — HIPS ACTION/SEPARATION

EXTENSION — FOLLOW-THROUGH — FINAL ROTATION

The Young Slugger's Guide to Hitting

CHAPTER 7: SWING SEQUENCE

Set Up

I start by evaluating the setup of the hitter. The setup is the foundation of the swing. It is critical that this step be done correctly and consistently, or everything built upon it will eventually fail.

During the setup phase, I am checking to see how the hitter approaches the plate. I check to see where they set up in relation to the plate. I measure the distance of their front foot from home plate. I do this to ensure they are standing in a consistent area, and have an accurate measuring system to ensure they stand as close as possible to the same place each time they step into the box.

I also measure the distance between their feet during setup. This step reveals consistency, balance and stride length. This is important because it helps me explain to my hitters why they need to maintain a strong, stable base.

The final aspect to the set up I am looking for is the bat angle. There is not a specific angle I seek here, but I am really looking to see the bat tilted over the head of the hitter with the knob pointing toward the catcher.

CHAPTER 7: SWING SEQUENCE

Load/Stride

During the load/stride aspect of the swing, I am evaluating the rhythm and timing of the hitter. I am looking for a confident move toward the ball, as they attack the ball with a controlled violence. We teach our hitters to swing with the intent to do damage. I will challenge them to swing as hard as they can while maintaining balance, and without falling over after the swing.

As they start the load/stride aspect, I check for a slight negative load or shifting of the weight from the center of the body to the back leg/back side. This weight shift is needed in order to create momentum with their forward movement. I need to see the hitters drive with their back leg, rather than "step to the pitcher" that our kids are often taught. This is where the swing begins. I teach my kids to start with the hips and the hands will follow. I stress the importance of this by giving them the verbal cue to "swing fast" with their hips not "swing hard" with their arms.

CHAPTER 7: SWING SEQUENCE

Foot Strike

When my hitters get to foot strike, which is the moment the front leg begins to bear weight, I am monitoring the drive they create from their back hip/leg. I will use a landmark in the background to show the separation. I will measure how far they drive away from that landmark.

I will measure the angle of the stride. I measure from the back toe-to the belt buckle-to the toe of the front foot. I am also looking to see if the front arm is still bent/relaxed. I also want to see the bat still cocked over the head of the hitter and the knob toward the catcher. This will create the hip/shoulder separation that we seek to create the greatest amount of force at impact.

CHAPTER 7: SWING SEQUENCE

Ignition

Ignition is what I call the first rotational move in the swing. The previous moves are made on every pitch, even in a non-swing. Ignition is when the hitter starts to move the bat towards impact. In this step I am checking to see when the hips start to open. I also note if the front foot lands open or closed.

I check the front arm action to see if it is straight or relaxed. I then look to see the angle of the bat, as it starts to leave the "cocked" position. I am looking for connection in the swing. I check to see if the hands go early, or if there is any arm barring/casting. I will stop my video, as the bat is vertical, to ensure that the body is still properly connected.

CHAPTER 7: SWING SEQUENCE

Hips Action/Separation

As the hitters enter the hip action phase of the swing, I am checking to see if the hips begin to open. For a right-handed hitter, their belt buckle will appear to be pointing at the second basemen. For a left-handed hitter, their belt buckle will appear to be pointing toward the short stop position. I also monitor the front arm to ensure it is pulling the knob through the zone. The bat path here is often where my younger hitters start to disconnect.

CHAPTER 7: SWING SEQUENCE

Knob to the Pitcher

The knob phase is the halfway point in the swing sequence. This is my favorite image, as you get to see the hitter in a unique position that you only see in slow motion. This checkpoint is one that all elite hitters hit on a regular basis. This image was made famous in Ted Williams book, *The Science of Hitting*.

This image, when viewed from the pitcher's perspective, only shows the knob of the bat. The barrel is hidden by the knob as the hitters are in mid rotation, and preparing to enter the hitting zone. This checkpoint reveals many issues.

At this phase, I monitor the back elbow to ensure it is tucked down into the back hip/rib area. I do not want to see the back elbow leading the bat through the zone. This flaw is known as bat drag, and will be covered in Chapter 8. It is also the number one flaw I see in younger hitters.

CHAPTER 7: SWING SEQUENCE

I am also monitoring the front arm to ensure it stays flexed as the shoulders rotate through the zone. We do not want to over extend the front arm until we get to impact. As for the lower half, you will see the belt buckle start to face the pitcher, and the back foot release and rotate towards the pitcher, as momentum is shifted from the back leg towards the front leg. For many years coaches would cue kids to squash the bug, but that is incorrect. If done correctly, the momentum will be generated from the back leg and transferred into the arms/front side at impact. If you google Bryce Harper, you will find that his back leg is off the ground at impact on the majority of his home runs.

Q: Why do we squash the bug?

A: We DO NOT squash the bug! In order to hit with power you must transfer the weight from the back foot to the front side. Think of your hitter as a video game with a power meter. In order to hit with the most power, we need to select the power meter at the moment of impact, where all of our energy is transferred from our body through our arms into the bat and out towards the ball.

#askcoachchris

CHAPTER 7: SWING SEQUENCE

Impact

The impact phase is the totality of the swing coming together. It is the moment that the bat and ball arrive at the point of collision with maximum force. Here, we need all of the energy generated to be transferred from our body through the bat and into the ball. At impact, I am looking to see if the arms are at or near extension. I check to see how far in front of the plate we are making impact. I also monitor the front leg action to ensure that it is firmly braced to give us our best foundation.

I want to see the head, hips and back knee in a vertical line. I use the cue "head-hips-knee." This is the axis for which our swing rotation happens. We need our rotational axis to be stationary in order to create the greatest amount of torque.

Many young sluggers end their drive at impact, but we still have energy left in our bodies and our bat that we must dissipate in a powerful manner. If you decelerate your bat prematurely, you will slow down your swing before impact.

CHAPTER 7: SWING SEQUENCE

Extension

Nearly all young hitters start to roll their wrist over at impact, and when they get to the extension phase, you will see both of their arms parallel to each other. At extension, I look for the arms to be in a Power V or stacked formation. I monitor the back foot to ensure that it has rolled over and releases from the ground. I should see the piping on the pants of this hitter as the back leg should rotate with the hips facing the pitcher.

I also make note of the shoulder turn to ensure it is still going around the axis of the swing.

CHAPTER 7: SWING SEQUENCE

Follow Through

In the final follow through of the swing, I note the timing of the wrist rolling over. I have not found a hard and fast rule to when is the right time. I just ensure that my hitters stay strong and rotate their shoulders through impact, as we arrive at the final rotation phase.

CHAPTER 7: SWING SEQUENCE

Final Rotation

When we get to the final rotation phase, I am looking for the hitters to rotate through and carry the shoulder rotation, so that their entire jersey is readable as they rotate around. I make a note to ensure their name or both digits are visible form my camera angle. This tells me that we have generated our maximum amount of power in the swing, and our body has decelerated the energy we created. If I am not getting this level of rotation, I know there is more power inside my hitter. Therefore, we start mining for it.

Chapter 8

Common Flaw Series

I have been coaching and training hitters for over twenty years, I have compiled a list of the most common flaws that I find in the hitters that come to me for help.

I will break down each of these issues, and show supporting images to help give the visual tools for you to help your slugger get started. I will also add some teaching tips, or coaching cues, to help them as they progress.

CHAPTER 8: COMMON FLAW SERIES

Feet

I start building all of my hitters from the ground up. A very common flaw I see with young hitters is their tendency to flare their back foot toward the catcher. I feel this is done because they feel like they can create more momentum with the open foot.

While they are correct about creating more momentum, they also leak true rotational power. I teach all of my hitters to set their back foot perpendicular to the catcher, so they can use the back foot to create a strong back wall. This will create leverage and increase ground force.

FLAW: Back foot flare out

CORRECT: Back foot perpendicular to pitcher

CHAPTER 8: COMMON FLAW SERIES

Knee

Another common flaw I see is the leaking of the back knee over the back foot. This creates for a very weak base, and causes a poor transition from the lower body to the upper body. Often, kids do not know they are doing this. The teaching point I use here is to have the kids get their foot set correctly (as in drill number 1). Then, have them set their back knee and put their weight on the instep of the back foot. Next, I ask them to slide their knee past their foot. As they do this, they will feel their base becoming weak, and understand the importance of keeping their weight in their instep.

FLAW: Knee leakage

CORRECT: Weight transfer to back leg instep

CHAPTER 8: COMMON FLAW SERIES

Shifting weight

I see kids shifting their weight improperly. They tend to slide back as they enter their load phase, shifting their weight to the outside of their foot. This creates a leaking of power. It will also lead to not getting the maximum energy from their swing. Proper lower body weight transfers, if done correctly, will greatly improve your slugger's performance and overall enjoyment of the game.

Lunging is one of the most noticeable flaws that hitters have from beginners to professionals. The coaching point I use for kids is a video game analogy. I ask the kids to think of playing a video game, and having a fireball as their weapon. This fireball sits on their back hip. The only way this fireball will deploy is by a fast rotation of the hips. As they drive their back hip toward the pitcher, the fireball deploys. The majority of sluggers understand this analogy, and it leads to greater rotational force.

FLAW: Lunging   **FLAW:** Leading with shoulders   **CORRECT:** Leading with hips

CHAPTER 8: COMMON FLAW SERIES

Rotation

There are many other flaws, and they are very difficult to show with pictures. I have been filming an online drill series that will be made available to all of my followers to ensure you are up to date with my coaching philosophies.

Counter rotation is when young sluggers load up by rotating towards the catcher. This motion is similar to the wind up they use to throw. They use this move in an attempt to generate more power, but it ultimately will create a timing issue. I don't mind for my hitters to have a little coil to their front shoulder. Counter rotation is the full closure of the hips during the loading phase.

FLAW: Counter rotation

CHAPTER 8: COMMON FLAW SERIES

Stride

The flaw of "stepping not driving" is one that I developed over a series of lessons with kids over striding. I found that they were using the coach's cue to "step toward the pitcher." I found that as my players would take that step toward the pitcher, they were getting flat in their hip and shoulder angles causing them to hit a high rate of ground balls. I then changed my cue from stepping to driving. Now I tell them to lift their front leg, and treat it like a kick stand. I want them to drive their back hip forward and push the front leg toward the pitcher. The correct image below shows the arrow at the point where they can "push the button" to move forward.

FLAW: Stepping not driving   **CORRECT:** Driving with the back hip

CHAPTER 8: COMMON FLAW SERIES

Collapse

Collapsing early on the back side is a very common flaw with young sluggers. They cave in their back side as they slide toward impact. This creates a weak swing, and often leads to swing and misses or soft pop ups. I often call this the "crazy banana" because my kids end up in the "reverse C" shape after they collapse. The "crazy banana" cue is one that they can have fun with as we fix it.

In order to fix collapsing, you need to stress the importance of rotating to contact and not sliding the hips through the hitting zone.

The front leg will collapse on young hitters who do not have proper movement patterns. The front leg is the brace that allows a hitter to transfer their weight and create maximum force at impact. If your slugger is struggling with a bent front leg work on keeping that leg straight as they land, so they can brace on it.

FLAW: Backside collapse

FLAW: Weak front leg

The Young Slugger's Guide to Hitting

CHAPTER 8: COMMON FLAW SERIES

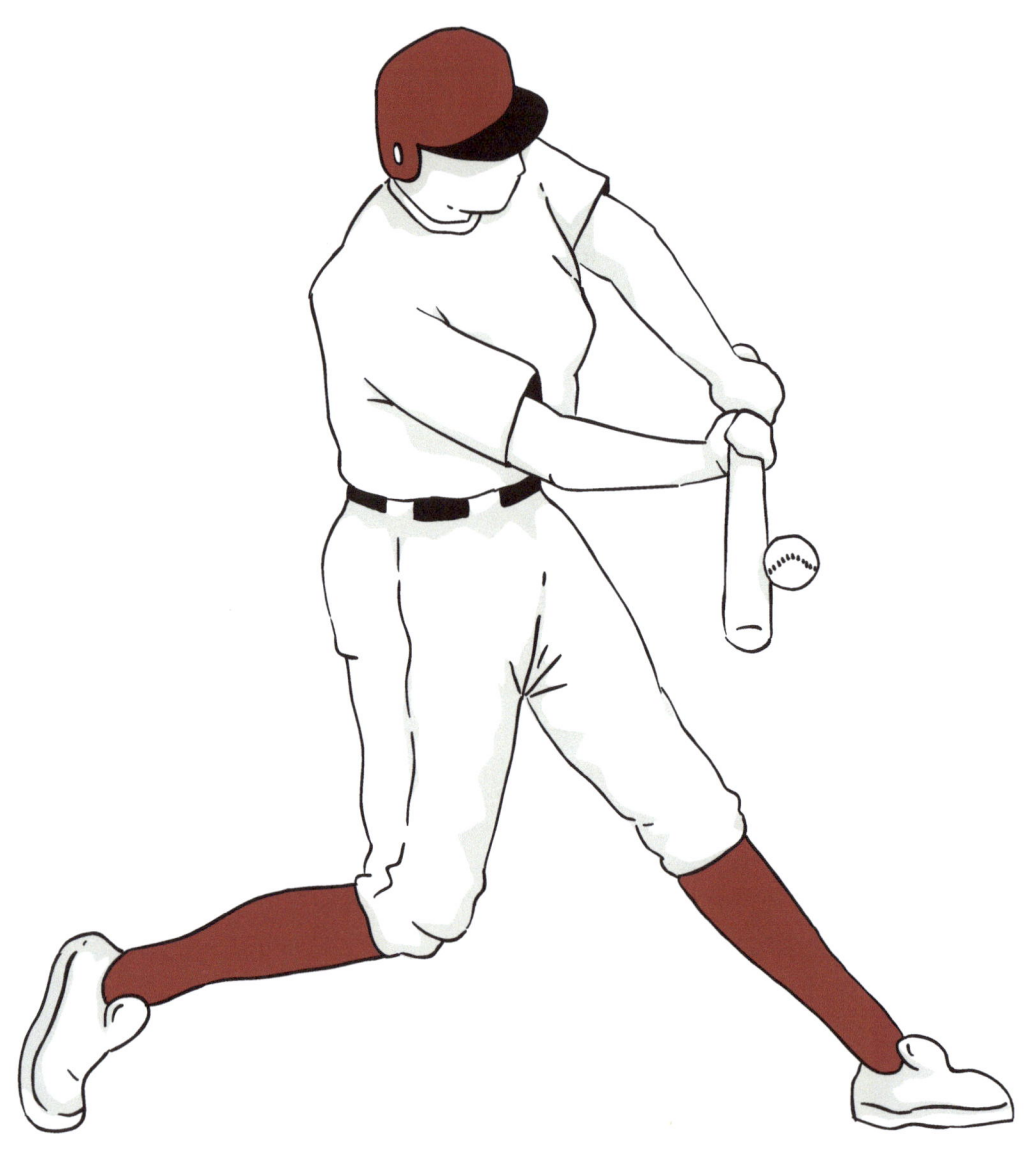

CORRECT: Straight front leg, head over hip over knee

CHAPTER 8: COMMON FLAW SERIES

Bat position

The once common feature that prolific hitters have in their swing is the bat position at foot strike. Every hitter has their bat tucked behind their head, and the knob pointing toward the catcher. They have the bat here, as their stride foot lands, creating the maximum amount of hip/shoulder separation.

FLAW: Improper bat position

FLAW: Improper bat position

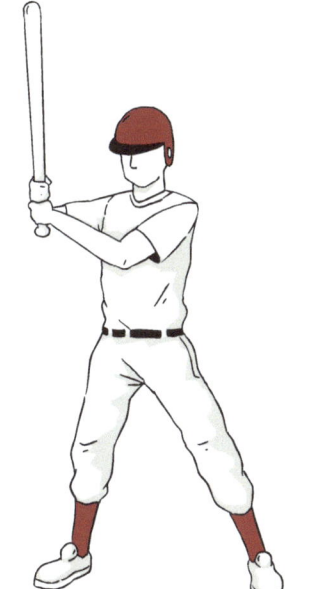

FLAW: Improper bat position

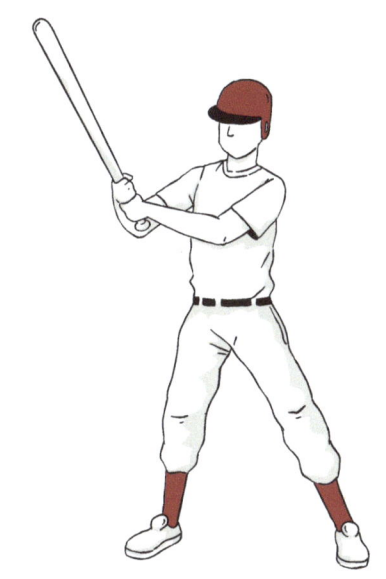

FLAW: Improper bat position

The Young Slugger's Guide to Hitting

CHAPTER 8: COMMON FLAW SERIES

CORRECT: Bat cock position

FLAW: Dropping hands

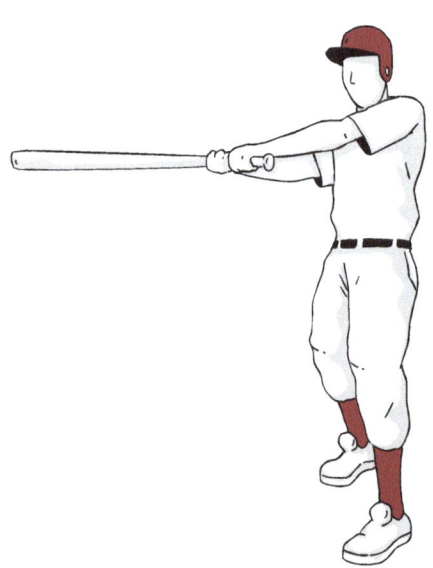

FLAW: Casting/arm barring

The Young Slugger's Guide to Hitting

Chapter 9
Mental Preparation

If you feel it, we can fix it.

The most under coached aspect of the game of baseball is the mental game. As I look back on my career and the highs and lows, it was my mental preparation that lead to my good days, and mental breakdowns that lead to failures.

I teach my hitters to develop an on deck routine as a way to clear out all of the negative thoughts, and get their mind focused on their next at bat. I train each of my hitters to perform a routine as a method to calm their mind and relax the tension in their body. It focuses on finding their breath and controlling their emotions. They must clear their head and have one final thought as they step into that box. The process I used as a player began once I put on my batting helmet. At that moment, I focus all my attention on my next at bat. I start while I am at least two hitters away from being at the plate. I will break it down in steps.

Q What do you tell kids to help focus?

A Visualize success. See the ball hitting the bat and landing in the grass. See it. Feel it. Do it.

CHAPTER 9: MENTAL PREPARATION

On Deck Routine

Step 1. I put on my helmet, and I check in mentally as to what my role will be at the plate. I observe the pitcher, the defense, and the sequence of the pitcher.

Step 2. Once I reach the on deck circle, I swing a weighted bat. I work on any specific swing flaws I am struggling with at the time. While doing this, I laser focus on the pitcher, looking for any weakness.

Step 3. As I step into the batter's box, I focus on the next pitch. I visualize the pitch I want to see and step in. I lock on to my zone, and wait for my pitch to hit.

The law of dominate thought states, "We become what we think about." If you are thinking negative thoughts, you will get negative results. Think positive thoughts.

CHAPTER 9: MENTAL PREPARATION

Q: What was your walk-up song?

A: I ask this question to my players, and am often met with a blank stare. It's obvious that many youth players don't have, or even understand the importance of, a walk-up song. Hitters who have a walk-up song understand that it is a critical element to their warm up routine. It gives them a sense of peace, as they tune out the noise and focus on the song. It allows their mind to escape the stress of the moment. It gives them confidence, as the song impacts their brain and removes all negative self-talk.

My walk-up song was "Hells Bells" by ACDC. I would stay on deck, and finish my routine during the church bells ringing. The bells rang for 25 seconds. This was my time. I put the game on hold, so I could focus on myself, within myself, and lock in on the next at bat. At the 25 second mark, the guitar would sound off, and I would slam the knob to the dirt, freeing the bat weight and make my way to the plate. It was time, and I was ready.

You should find your own walk-up song. Find a song that speaks to you, motivates you, and gives you confidence. If you are not able to play with walk-up music, listen to it in your pregame and on your way to the game. When you step on deck, turn on the music in your mind and get your jam on!

#wheelhousebaseball #askcoachchris
#practiceonpurpose #trusttheprocess #practice

Chapter 10
Practice Habits

Practice on Purpose

Quality over Quantity. I encourage you to limit the number of swings in a young slugger. Your body will start to tire after just 3-4 swings, and then your body makes adjustments for fatigue, minor adjustments you will not notice. If you take 15-20 swings in a row with the goal of creating muscle memory, you are doing just that, but bad muscle memory.

I encourage my players not to take more than three swings in a row without stepping out of the box and regrouping, both physically and mentally. Mindless swings are a waste of time, and make your success more difficult to obtain. If you take ten swings per day from the beginning of your tee ball career, by the time you graduate high school, you will have 51,100 quality swings under your belt, just from this 10 swings per day method.

#askcoachchris

Q How much should I practice?

A If you take ten swings per day from age 5 to your senior year, you will have 51,100 quality swings under your belt.

CHAPTER 10: PRACTICE HABITS

We have all heard the 10,000 hours or reps rule. If you start with a solid foundation and build on that foundation with 51,100 bricks, you will have an amazing foundation for success. I cannot promise success, but I can promise you will have a love for the game and a work ethic that will be rivaled by few. That work ethic will translate into all aspects of life.

If it matters, measure it. Keep a journal to track progress. It will keep you motivated. Always be honest with yourself. When you lie to yourself in practice, everyone will know when it comes game time.

#askcoachchris

Q How do you track your progress?

A My saying is, "If it matters, measure it." I encourage you to keep a journal to track your progress. It won't happen overnight, so stay patient and keep grinding.

Chapter 11
Training Aids

Launch Pad Swing Trainer

During my time as a coach, I converted from a low line drive mentality to driving the ball with the intent to do damage. During that conversion, I conducted a launch angle study of some of Major League Baseball's greatest hitters. I will share some of the highlights, but the results of that study were amazing, and can be found at www.launchpadswingtrainer.com.

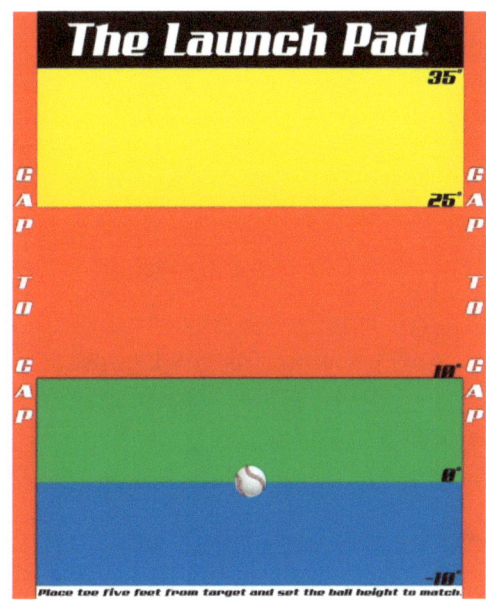

CHAPTER 11 : TRAINING AIDS

Launch Angle

Launch angle represents the vertical angle at which the ball leaves a player's bat after being struck.

- **Ground Ball:** Less than 10 degrees
- **Line Drive:** 10-25 degrees
- **Fly Ball:** 25-50 degrees
- **Pop Up:** Greater than 50 degrees

Generally, pitchers who can limit their launch angle against (keeping the ball on the ground) are more successful, because they are the most adept at avoiding home runs and extra-base hits, which come almost exclusively via fly balls and line drive. Average launch angle tells us about the tendencies of hitters, too — with a high average launch angle indicating a fly-ball hitter, and a low average launch angle indicating a ground-ball hitter. On average, fly-ball hitters generally drive in more runs than ground ball hitters do.

Exit Velocity

Exit velocity is defined as the speed of a baseball after a batter hits it. This includes all-batted ball events — outs, hits and errors. Attaining a high exit velocity is one of a hitter's primary goals. A hard-hit ball will not always have a positive result, but the defense has less time to react. Therefore, the batter's chances of reaching base are higher.

Major League Baseball Results

- **Bryce Harper:** This slugger is a generational talent. The third youngest player ever to win the Most Valuable Player Award. His launch angles tell an amazing story. The slugger had a .535 average on balls leaving the bat between 11-25 degrees. Of his 42 home runs, 19 of them came from the 25-degree launch angle. At 25 degrees, the MVP hit .806 (29 for 36) with 19 home runs.
- **Miguel Cabrera:** This slugger has been the model of consistency for many years. A career average of .321, 446 home runs and over 1500 RBIs. This monster is the last hitter to win the Triple Crown. Every hitter has a sweet spot, and Miggy is no exception. At a launch angle of 10 degrees, he has an average of .889! He was 24 for 27 at bat balls struck at a 10-degree launch angle.

In closing, I want to extend my deepest gratitude for your support, and hope that I will continue to be a trusted resource for you and your slugger as they develop throughout their career.

Conclusion

I hope you have found this guide useful in many ways. I encourage you to trust your child, and their feel as you implement these changes. Allow them to try their own way, let them look at the photos and experiment. The Young Slugger's Guide to Hitting is a simplified process for parents and coaches to help build consistant swings. Each step is important, and allow the kids to work though the process and find success.

I hope you enjoyed the Young Slugger's Guide to Hitting. I hope that you implement it with your child, your team or any kid you see on the verge of giving up. I want to be an ongoing resource for you and your slugger.

The greatest compliment you can give me is to share my information with someone else. Please log in and provide a book review. Visit our website and share your success story.

Most importantly, get out there and have fun!

www.ingramcontent.com/pod-product-compliance
Lightning Source LLC
Chambersburg PA
CBHW042002150426
43194CB00002B/95